Heliotropes

La Presse 2008
Iowa City & Paris

Heliotropes

Ryoko Sekiguchi, translated by Sarah O'Brien

Heliotropes copyright © 2005 P.O.L
Translation copyright © 2008 Sarah O'Brien
All rights reserved

Published in the United States by La Presse, an imprint of Fence Books

La Presse/Fence Books are distributed by University Presses of New England.
www.upne.com
www.lapressepoetry.com

Library of Congress Control Number 2008925114
Sekiguchi, Ryoko
Heliotropes by Ryoko Sekiguchi, translated by Sarah O'Brien
p.   cm.

ISBN 978-1-934200-20-9

1. French poetry.   2. Poetry.   3. Contemporary translation.

First Edition
10 9 8 7 6 5 4 3 2 1

This book was first published in French in 2005 by P.O.L;
we would like to thank Paul Otchakovsky-Laurens and the author
for graciously granting us permission to publish this translation.

Heliotropes

There's an entire system of pronunciation shored up by the Latin names of plants and what they're staked against. From a structure to the left and out of what might, in a moment of distraction, be called "its contents," something emerges – an extension, which must stream clear without adding extra weight. The distinction between passive and active voices was instantly forbidden, and barely a glance toward the third, the letter f had already appeared; we pronounced it; the same thing happened to us.

We did everything we could to hold the overflow back, but we all knew that nothing could prevent the surge. In a season that takes note of the sectors turning green one after the other, everyone was handed a piece of light yellow paper on which the words *Jardim botânico* or *Jardim tropical* stood out; birds don't read, its back door opening directly onto another botanical garden.

While each bird's
spiral or ascent is
set, inalterable, and
their instinctual flight
patterns predeter-
mined, plants, which
can't go anywhere
alone, are allowed only
oscillation; they con-
stantly sway and fold.

Formed for life, the front edge is especially thick and full, sharpening toward the back, shaped like a blade. You'll notice that the bottom is flat or sometimes slightly concave, becoming fuller again toward the top, to smooth the flow of air.

From out here, we can only imagine how to untangle the space inside and have no way of matching them up with their classifications, but we can, at least, begin with the simple names we already know. This is how we determine that they're mostly composed of salt, sulfur, and other important components, such as coal and ash, and that in with the compounds are relatively pure things, such as water, air, and silicate, or to put it simply, kinds of stone, various plants, and creatures that move.

No two here have the same name, and if sometimes they seem very close, the next syllable pronounced distances them from certain species while linking them with still others in an ever-ascending stair, a digital landscape that continues to unfurl.

The name wasn't hidden at all – in fact, it was carefully copied out right beside each one, but when it's not clear what's being named or exactly what is included, the gesture seems random, and once, in error, everything that breathes, belong to the black poplar family, or has an uneven surface was lumped together. Anything with variable leaves, or arrow-shaped – anything from the cotton genus, semi-winged, or branching out all over; by mixing up half-named, partly-formed flowers, and not knowing why, at times, he too cocks his head at the shrubbery.

A thin layer of leaves
swirled around inside,
mapping shifts in the
currents of air. Tracing
irregular flights, arching
the whole body, the
back gently turning, the
point of the support-
ing foot served as a
brief tangent between
contact and leap.

If it doesn't flower
for awhile, we can't
name it, so we leave
it there, a bare noun,

Heading back over the hill to the path, I noticed a bright yellow flower bed that I hadn't seen before. In a clearing that later became a landmark, I looked down and saw something sticking out behind the writing. Having come from a country farther south whose name begins with a light, plosive consonant, this phrase barely uttered, the birds whose necks are stained with the same yellow flew off in a racket, calling *lepp / pod / bur / caffra / rip / ot / ka* – names obscured as one cry muffled another – they performed their circular flight.

From Aleppo, from Podolia
or the one with the petioled
leaves, from Liburnia, from
Kaffraria, the one who
remains on shore, from
elsewhere, from Arkansas,

As if matching early summer's strong sunlight, the
half-shadowed space parallels the walk, and the
metallic tarnish glares so that we can't see inside;
the branches bending to the curve of the dome
bring to mind a time and tense spoken only in
the past, but after coming around to the front, its
height – almost fifty feet – upends expectations,
and in the greenhouse, in the diffuse light that
erases the layered shadows under trees so
enormous that they now grow only downward,
unable to disentangle their branches, far from
comparing the nameplates with the leaves.

Simply put, the differing
rates of growth and
changes in pressure that
expand the surround-
ing cells provoke these
openings and closings,
violent contractions, a
rise in temperature, or a
slight inclination of the
bust; there is no other
possible   hypothesis.

This being that spends most of its life wrapped in air, almost unable to walk on land, has developed the tendency to catch *liquid* consonants in a burst of stationary flight, then rush off. So the sounds of ل and ر are mostly left out, and know nothing of the life of plants under crown cover, of the vigor of tree trunks, or of the luxuriance of the underbrush, and – never clearly heard – they are left to evaporate.

Out of fear of leaving it unidentified, many names, sometimes up to a dozen, are given to a single thing. The plant whose name begins with a *d*, with three acute angles, has been called granite-lover, the blood-colored, that-which-stands-straight, that-which-beds-down-in-the-earth, it-from-the-Caucasus, and several other things; it was the look of its leaves, as if it had forgotten that plants can travel with the aid of their names, as if the name remained only for those who were looking right at it.

On the skin of
an indicative plant,
without straying
from the dyed part
of the plate, still
in the category of
that which the sun
hits, they take up a
glottal vibration as
each odd number
arrives, which some
beings would find
difficult, yet they
devote themselves
to repeating it.

The Latin names
of plants, however
long they take to
say, all have exactly
the same weight.

In a fairly hilly place, where humidity rises off the
water, going with the others always meant taking
the longest route, and then, throughout the day,
we watch them trying to catch the air's currents,
and locking their gaze, choose the longest smooth
glide among the possible courses; we see how
they underscore a tangent in order to map it. At
dusk, as though testing it out, each one following
its chosen route, the voiced, as if calling a meeting,
buzzed loudly; we're amazed at the effect of
the soundboards placed all around the inside.

Why do some keep
pushing, up or out,
sometimes at ground
level or beneath, while
others, to avoid being
fixed in space, fly with
out thinking of land,

The opened ground
calls to mind the layering
of space, suggesting
an overflow of super-
imposed occasions,

After the second colonization, one flowerbed offers itself up for minute and silent observation, refusing to be addressed over and over by different names. Eyes can't see the whole plant at once, nor do they attempt to understand the physical nature of death by wilting; simply the alternating warming and cooling, which happens every year, and so they repeat it.

We do not settle for song. With every breath, consonants drop to the bottom of the throat, and instantly get cast up again by the syrinx; we can even have a long conversation at four am that includes sounds such as ب and ف.

The sound of the call reaches the birds,
and the whistler faithfully imitates the
beak's cadences without understanding
the language he's speaking; from the
foliage, another voice calls back; the
bird's response is not always understood,
consonants uttered to follow vowels, and
vowels follow other vowels, making the
center of life out of something like a flood
or circuit – no one doubted it at the time.

This instrument, which is used as a hammer, a chisel, and gardening shears, as a key, a lance, and sometimes a basket or sieve, is also at times used to communicate. It's something like a wave, its splendid crest and descent; it also protects a body always in motion.

After climbing up for a clearer view, we saw the
landscape fanning down toward the river, not in a
gentle slope but in terraces, and a colony of climbing
plants – as if to envelop a field of other living things –
covered the ground, completely, with indigo flowers.
Hadn't it considered other ways of reaching water, the
green billowed and tumbled toward shore, tracing the
precise contours of the landscape and everything on
it, the bird also unfurling along this line, a little above.

Plants of un-
certain aspect
putting   the
place in scale,

We felt the rush of the ف wind here too,
and despite the buckling and rustling of the
branches, it easily lands on an impossibly steep
twig, while it throws the other foot in the air
as if in a hammock, saying: "They exist at a
distance from every language spoken today on
earth, while each one points in a single, precise
direction. It's like this in all gardens, anywhere
that flight is the preferred mode of travel."

Alone, slowly, but
always effortlessly,
it glides through
tiny interstices, its
shadow now diagonal
across this space.

Crossing a spot where once a grove of thin-branched trees had stood, their wings suddenly stutter, shudder on their axes, though they don't actually encounter a thing, then beat even harder to regain their composure. No one would notice this "flailing phenomenon" unless intently observing, and it only applies to birds smaller than four centimeters; they say the bigger ones dial this slender space of interruption back to zero by stirring up a vaster area with their avian muscles.

Were we going to grow this year's plumage on the backs of those who are no longer here, or are those who are no longer here dividing their roots behind us,

What is the life of the
thin overlaid leaves that
loosen their own skin right
up to the edge of the still
young shoot, and in split-
ting open reveal a swath of
palisade tissue, which the
sound *i* slightly interrupts,

Once done phonating, they have no reason to stay up so high; they dive, revealing the symmetry of their flight feathers. An instant later, the ب sound falls in pelting rain, echoes among the aerial roots, amplifying the metallic resonance; we say the drops will never reach the ground.

The cherimoya can simply skip the step that produces its netting-covered fruit, in which case the birds also stay away, not that they'd kept an eye on it before. What is the relationship between one change conjured by another, the fact that water doesn't cling to plants, and the way the drinking bird is inverted, and what is the relationship between this and the fact that the image of water never leaves the heart and that the word "humidity" is covered in down? This is not yet known.

As if trying to slip through, they peered in;
they wanted to get close to the plants, having
already skimmed the words that fall between,
bending closer and facing the object in order
to name it. To draw out the pronunciation for
as long as possible, so that the terms of the
species keep repeating, troubling the distinc-
tion between the noun and the sentence.

Nepeta wears flowers pedunculated at intervals, shaped like
spears, the cucurbitaceae's lobed leaves resemble those of
the bitter apple, black seeds, carnation with unisex flowers,
with short calyxes, partial ovals, and notched corollas,

On this clearly
bounded earth,
only birds call
plants by their
own   names,

Setting out from the *Botanical Garden* and all that lives there, if green spreads over the page we are not given, which of the four of us retains this landscape?

Personal pronouns inter-
weave to conform to the
proliferation of albumen,

Otherwise certain
animals can be
mimed, and as he
closes the distance,
he discretely with-
draws from the
landscape. This is
how we got close,
bound inexorably by
the atmosphere, like
those that decom-
pose the same way.

Because the tops of the trees kept brushing against the bars, the light in the big aviary seemed more vivid than natural light. The birds at the water's edge lived there, and from time to time went through their awkward paces. But more than just the captive birds are here, the wild uncounted, the grayish-brown, slipping in unthinking, who come to peck at food not meant for them, how do they bend their wings; they flit effortlessly here and there through the smaller bars, and we are struck at every instant by this glinting transit; it's as if the bars have disappeared.

I am the one
who anchors
it   for   now.

While water doesn't exactly promise a calming circulation, in terms of the commute and the leap, nothing is better; the flowers of the bird of paradise are a good example. On the hillside to the east, thanks to volcanic sedimentation and water erosion, the wind stirred limbs sixty feet high, and water particles that had been lifted up above the current confused the heights of the leaves and floated between, turning the tops of the trees into atmosphere. Here, in the hot season, it rained a lot, and into the afternoon, its fog.

Not only calling those
who paused here, but
also those they sought,
to go on like this,

50

Owning either to the sunlight or the plant-life,
it is covered by a leaf-laden canopy that you
only have to glance up to recognize; it hides
the shadows of the small things that live there,
but still lets the fresh air in so that the nest
never stagnates; and as a brief exception, it
could have lived alongside the pronunciations:
beginning with an *l*, begun by a *t,* an *r* rolling
in the middle, a little longer, playing against
a *u,* a *k,* and a *d,* sometimes considering a ش,
inviting a ك, gently leaning its beak toward a
م, or a pronouncement that finishes with a ن.

Normally the image lingers
on the retina, creating
an unbroken scene in a
constantly blinking eye,
but in the observed field
this balance is easily
jostled – the nictitating
eyelids stay open, scenes
don't correspond, are crop-
ped, and the Jerusalem
thorn, which even under
a steady gaze seemed
only a heap of points,
fills out its whole span.

While we don't really
know what gets lost
or what slips away,
in winter they all
escape underground;
nothing disappears
in the tropics, and
where one humming-
bird flags, another
species of hum-
mingbird emerges,

This irregular chirping
isn't meant to claim
territory, or signal food,
or attract a mate – it's
meant to keep this rare
sound in the throat,

As if trying to carry the tune of a slow, deep breath, the parallel-veined leaves were ready to lean forward on their own – we were crouching down right in front of them. Through the flickering of these things and the light coming up behind, it tried again to be grafted.

We felt that passing through the exact same place time and again created a one-way current in the air, swaying like hands, like cilia. Still in the same place, in the sensitive hours, the sharp folioles that don't belong to the marbled leaves displayed a double edge in profile; you only had to look down to notice it. And the sun that hit the skin, as if overtaking the radiated field, extended down close to the ground from one side of its arc; the other side spread into the air, and for the first time, the plants treated this quick curving interstice like an opening in space, and the instrument answered it like an eye.

So that it should
be carried away
by a minor sepal,

If I don't look twice at the stiff rectrix between the crowns of the yellow laurel rose, if I don't pick it up with my right hand, I could go the whole year without noticing the sudden changes of plumage. A green feather verging on yellow could have been the glint off a flower; its barbs, almost feathers themselves, grow parallel from the barbules that clasp each other and pluck at the corollas. Unable to catch the feathers that keep decomposing into microscopic dust, if wings carry birds, and if the names give us the feathers that carry them, if they give them to us no matter what, the steaming heat that has risen to the throat remains for a moment.

To   take   flight   you
don't need to lean on
the left foot, which is
already in the air, or
to push off on tiptoe,

Often real motion escapes detection by the unaided eye, but when we peer at the ground or at the little plants, we're able to pick it out by a gleam that skims over the top layer of greenery, by an awkward rustling of leaves, or by something like a presence we can't quite place, or simply by its song. Even with our eyes closed we felt the shadow thrown over the objects, and the bridge used to extend the landscape or the heights; I already knew when we mentioned the shadow that the tropical garden exists for those who cross it parallel.

Even though the branches seem to throw open their arms as we walk between the trees, we manage to convince ourselves otherwise by reasoning that it's a question of angle, and that this is just one of thousands of possible results (they could have also grown upward), but where the road curves once we've reached the crest, the branches stretch overhead to create a sparse screen of interruption before our eyes, formed of parallel lines with extended arms, to be in the heart of a landscape takes you out of the ordinary, as if to say they were coming back.

Things we thought already gone end up in the shadow
of bland shrubs that we don't picture in the tropics,
in the shadow of lush brazilwood and jimson weed,
and once we notice them, they swirl up and pour out
in waves from behind, insisting on a response. From
now on, they will never stop, not for the gaze that is
never the same, nor for the fact that despite yourself,
you read aloud, nor for closing time, above all now
that the days have gotten long, nor for the birds'
nighttime schedule, when everything comes out again.

If the twisting differs, the shadow that shares its firing angle, which hasn't concerned us until now, becomes "the front-comer," which is often deflected by beings whose eyelids close from the bottom, and like all *vacillating forms,* including sweltering heat and scintillating patterns, bends unevenly backward and forward by fixing its principal axis at its feet, suddenly arching its bust against the call.

Already dispersed,
they scatter toward
how many differ-
ent   destinations,

Again a moment on the edges of life: the colors vanish, and after
this sign, description becomes a prairie echo; again and again
the wind sweeps over us, distance doubles, as does the possible
volume of our voice across the land, becoming solid as it moves,

Just where this turning
overleaf was supported,
the middle finger or the
shadow of a wingtip,
which, placed on a back
arched in its momentum,
had until then created
this thin distance, now
leaves its post. The talon
is mindful of parabolic
movement, thin leaves
scattered between them;
it was going to put
them back in order.

These creatures that
do everything with
their lips, so to speak,
what they skim,

In the field of vision, the water temper-
ature rises from the side that forms the
circle. If it curls up all at once, the tension
of the pericarp grows, feet pitched to
the stage of dilation where it's already
too late to draw back. In this instance lit
red without a source of light, the waist
extremely thin, it mimics watery or aqueous
fruits, which gives it its transparence.
I was expecting it, straightening up.

Following the curve of the cambium layer that forms the bole
between phloem and wood after many years, a thin grid of light
marks the growing point, even if we can only take it in with our eyes,

After their names had been called once, after an interval of
time and distance, they appear today as a vaporous body,

They surround spectacles that
dissipate as they increase, and
can go on forever, yet some-
how still belong to the present,

Like many of the
red flowers that
bloom on tropical
trees, these are also
pollinated by birds,

Without changing
the form of the
rhyme to the end,

Barely   holding
on   by   a   lone
left   hand,   they
also   clasp   it,

Oscillation travels through air, acting
on the consonants, a slight shudder
reaching those with names. Names
never spoken aloud are now passed
on to the birds, who drag the entire
system of pronunciation along with
them, a system that never voiced
them, but only talked around them.
The birds guided them toward what
had to be their last stop; seated on
countless tree limbs, leaning forward,
an opportunity to offer their beaks
and to call the name appearing next,

This stoma
takes a form
we can no
longer read,

Now the entire system of pronunciation gets
left in the hands of the Latin names of plants,
and the same thing happened to us, rushing at
what we call the constant current or the table of
contents, *Cycas circinalis, Erythrina abyssinica, Punica
granatum, Parkinsonia aculeate, Annona cherimola,
Gossypium herbaceum, Thevetia Peruviana, Duranta
repens, Justicia brandegeana, Ipomoea cairica, Datura
sanguinea, Brassaia actinophylla, Asclepias curassavica,
Acacia caffra, Delonix regia, Cycas circinalis.*

This project was born in 2001, in the tropical gardens of Portugal. Of its seventy blocks, eleven were written in the summer of 2002 in Paris and England, five in October 2003 in Paris, and the rest, between January 7 and May 31, 2004, in both French and Japanese. An ongoing correspondence with the sculptor Isamu Wakabayashi (1936-2003) was seminal to this project at every stage. Sometimes he sent drawings along with his letters, at other times, his texts on nature. I would very much have liked to hear his ideas – which remain very much with us – on this book.

Some of its phrases are altered versions of lines taken from books of botany and ornithology, particularly from *How Plants Get Their Names* by Liberty Hyde Bailey (Macmillan, 1933). (Translator's note: This text was not consulted in the translating process, and no phrases in this translation are taken from any other books.)

This book is also my response to the "Muwashshah," a poetic form that was popular in the Arabic Andalusia of the Middle Ages, and in particular, to its final line, which is called "kharja." I hope that this text, rooted deep in the Iberian Peninsula, will be worthy of those earlier poets who managed to invent a form still able to fill us with awe.

And I would like to thank the French Centre national du livre most warmly for the grant that made this book possible; I'd also like to thank the literary journal *Vacarme,* which published a portion of this text. My warm thanks also to Alexandre Papas and Justine Landau for their attentive reading of and suggestions on this work, and to Daniel Heller-Rosen, whose writings on "the end of the poem" first brought the "Muwashshah" to my attention.

Ryoko Sekiguchi was born in Tokyo and moved to Paris in 1997, where she studied art history at the Sorbonne. She received her doctorate in comparative literature in 2000 from the University of Tokyo, then returned to Paris, where she currently lives and teaches at various institutions including the Paris Research Center for Oriental Languages and Civilizatons. She has published seven books of poetry in Japanese and seven in French, most recently *Heliotropes* (P.O.L) and *Adagio ma non troppo* (le Bleu du ciel). Other work of hers is available in English in the Litmus/Belladonna Press volume *Four From Japan* and in *Two Markets, Once Again* translated by Sarah Riggs and published by Post Apollo Press. She has collaborated with visual artists, including Suzanne Doppelt and Christian Boltanski, and the sound artist Rainier Lericolais. She translates poetry, prose, and criticism from Dari, French, and Japanese. She lives and works in Paris.

Sarah O'Brien was born in Ohio and received her BA from Brown University and her MFA from the Iowa Writers' Workshop. She has worked as a baker, photographer, and translator, and has traveled widely, spending time in South America, South Africa, South-east Asia, and Europe. Her poems and translations have appeared in *eXchanges, Columbia: A Journal of Literature and Art,* and *eleven/eleven*. She is currently teaching in France.

This is the third title in the La Presse series of contemporary French poetry in translation. The cover image is a page from the original P.O.L publication with holographic notes made by the translator. This series is edited by Cole Swensen and designed by Shari DeGraw. This book is set in Sumner Stone's Magma Light.